I0530347

Soulfull Thoughts

Mary O'Neill

Copyright © 2024 by Mary O'Neill

Paperback: 978-1-964744-10-0
eBook: 978-1-964744-11-7
Library of Congress Control Number: 2024911872

All rights reserved. No part of this publication may be reproduced,
distributed, or transmitted in any form or by any electronic or
mechanical means, without the prior written permission of the publisher,
except in the case of brief quotations embodied in critical reviews and
certain other noncommercial uses permitted by copyright law.

Ordering Information:

Prime Seven Media
518 Landmann St.
Tomah City, WI 54660

Printed in the United States of America

Contents

SOULFULL THOUGHTS

True salvation is freedom from negativity, and above
all from past and future as a psychological need.
https://www.**eckharttolle**.com/

1. Miracles

Yes I believe in miracles,
the miracle of every baby born
that goes to make the human race,
all the seeds sown that become
trees stout and strong,
the tides that come and go
conducted by the moon,
the sun that gives light and heat
and colours so bright
and together with the rain
that gathers in the clouds,
grows the food we eat.
The human brain -
the master of ingenuity
and author of technology.
The mountains and the rivers,
the sea that laps at every shore.
The bark of the dog and bleat of sheep,
the animals in the wild,
whose wisdom beggars belief.
The bees that buzz in the noonday sun.
the smell of a rose,
bird song at dawn and golden sunset.

Yes I believe in miracles
and could go on and on.

2. Daffodils

Fresh green shoots open
leaves silently unfurl
time of life and hope.
Yellow daffodils trumpet
long days and sunshine.

3. The Plovers

The rain filled clouds
in the menacing winter sky,
hung down to meet
the shrouded mountain
and the climbing forest.
The slender morning sun
made glistening gems
of a flock of plovers
swooping and soaring
in their exotic dance.

Suddenly the clouds cleared,
but I stood stock still,
spellbound by the beauty
and magic of the scene.

4. A Falling Star

A full moon shines in a clear starry sky,
everything is still and quiet,
a field mouse scurries in dry leaves.
Mars, Venus, Jupiter
the Milky Way and countless stars
sparkle and twinkle like fairy lights.
Suddenly a star falls,
as I watch the shower of sparkling shards,
I make a wish -
that everyone I know and love
can experience a moment like this.

5. Heartsease

Viola Tricolour so brave and true.
it doesn't face the sky,
but looks you in the eye,
with a perky prancing dance,
clad in the colour of kings,
the sunshine kissing its lips,
each one standing so close,
yet not crowding or crushing,
the more you take,
the more it has to give.
Just to look at the little flower
can ease the ache in your heart.

6. The Glen

The rising trees cast stark shadows in the deep glen,
the rain moistened leaves in glorious autumn colours
of russet, amber, gold and brown,
glisten as they gracefully drift to the ground.
From a small blue patch in the dark grey sky,
the brilliant afternoon sun shines,
framed by dazzling white cloud,
making everything green greener still.
Rock and road shimmer like silver,
every shape and shade intensified.
Here and there where cloud permits,
heavenly shafts beam down,
creating a cameo of contrasts
dim and bright
dark and light
alive and dead
sad and soul stirring –
all indelibly signed by God.

7. *Water*

Water is God's most precious gift
to man and earth,
it flows, falls, swamps, seeps and floods.
But without it our world
would be a scorched barren plain,
no grass, no trees, no flowers, no fruit,
no birds, bees, cows, fish or elephants,
no soil, no clouds or sea shore
and of course no us.
Diamonds the biggest player in earthly wealth
fade into insignificance
beside this shimmering sparkling
staff of all life,
honoured since time began
and now seriously endangered by man.

What will it serve us
to have day trips to the moon
if every drop we drink is suspect,
polluted by the sum of all burnt fossil fuels
that rise to rain on all we eat and drink
and other noxious chemicals and fumes
that wend their way to pollute
the water in the crystal mountain stream,
the vast expanse of oceans,
the rain that falls from the sky,

and the underground stream.
So that which was once so pure
all bear the brunt of man's advances.
We put money time and energy to conserve,
meter, bottle, filter and purify,
moving ever further from water as it was.
Can we win the race?
Can we reverse the poisonous waste?

8. Spring Leaves

And during the busyness of the day
when we fail to see
second by second unnoticed unseen,
the tiny pregnant buds swell and grow
and ever so gently unfurl,
until the winter's ghostly sceptres
of brown bare twigs
are miraculously adorned
by the most spectacular garb,
of a myriad of shades and shapes
of leaves and blooms so fresh,
to give us a countryside
all decked in spring best.

9. Among The Beech And Oak

Among the beech and oak
all dressed in autumn glory
I sit and ponder in sombre mood
what God had planned for man.
It's true nature has its brutality
with hurt pain and sadness,
but nothing to remotely compare
with mans' inhumanity to man.

Pharmaceutical companies selling sickness,
ozone damage with gas emissions,
nuclear stations that can wipe out nations
and wars where people do not count.

Mans' ingenuity has scaled such heights,
landing on the moon and climbing Everest,
global communication and instant information,
but in totality can we measure the gain?

What will it benefit man
if in the race to gain,
the very basics of existence
are lost to generations not yet born?

The swallows in Autumn migrate
the squirrels gather nuts

and the sparrow seed and soft fruit
all with man their greatest threat.

Man could take a closer look at nature
and learn from its wisdom so infinite,
also peruse the treasures lost
that our forefathers lived each day.

10. Grass

A blade of grass
delicate and green,
so forgiving of being cut
or being trampled underfoot,
gives us the carpet,
soft even to a baby's touch,
of rich green fields,
the roadside verge,
lawns and parks.
When let grow it gently
wafts in the breeze,
it drapes our ditches.
and nurtures our animals,
a soft place for them
to lie and chew their cud,
and sleep well at night,
while the hay and silage
stand them in good stead
in the long cold winter.
and all the while
its seeds and roots
grow and multiply.

11. The Bee

The bee with its brown stripy body,
silvery clear wings and distinctive buzz,
is feared by some for its sting,
but thanked by more for its honey,
which even for some
can help when pollen is a problem.
It gives rise to 'Busy as a bee'
and a 'Hive of Industry'.
Sayings based on how
things work within the colony.
Worker bees leave the hive
and travel miles to collect the pollen,
then laden they return
and in a most complex way,
convert that pollen into honey.
This they store in waxen honeycomb,
from there it goes into the jar
and onto the supermarket shelf.

12. The Seeds

The flower is now dead
withered and gone,
that once gave such delight.
Its beauty was balm to the senses
in shape colour and smell.
But in its dying form
the promise of life is already there,
where once the petals bloomed,
now brown and drooping,
tiny seeds slowly develop.
When the winter winds are blowing
these beacons of life
will bide their time until it's spring,
then to the world they will give
the joy and beauty of
the plant and flower once again.

13. Unique Qualities

Every plant that grows
down to the humble blade of grass
is truly a constant source
of wonder and amazement,
but should you chance to ask me
to choose between the daisy and the rose
I could well say......

The daisy is one of the most insignificant
and smallest of the flowers,
it grows under foot
and its petals close at dusk,
its roots grow rampantly in the lawn
and no matter how I dig
they soon will be back again.

The rose it has thorns
that can prick to the quick,
its petals fall to the ground
and make a mess,
it needs constant spraying
for greenfly black spot and mildew,
and if not pampered and pruned,
roses quickly outgrow themselves.

The daisy with its bright white petals
and sunny golden core,

makes such a pretty soft carpet
sprinkled in the green grass,
when trod upon
it just stands right back up
as if untouched.
Centuries of children have
made daisy chains
and how would lovers ever know
whether they were loved or not
if they did not have daisy petals to pluck?

No garden can be complete without
the splendour of a rose bush
whose heady perfume intoxicates
and lasts a lifetime of memory.
The velvety sensual feel of the petals
and the range of colour are so special
and how better can a lover say
'I love you'
than with a bunch of red roses?

So please don't ask me to choose
'cos each has qualities so unique
and the good of each
far outweighs the bad
and the same goes
for every human we know.

14. Mother Earth

Oh Mother Earth
I approach with reverence and awe,
you and that which you bring forth
from your soft brown soil,
so generously endowed
from your abundance
and in spite of man's disregard
for the delicate balance
of the miracle of your being,
with true mother love you provide
the endless complex constituents
that support my humble
but even more complex being.
In thankfulness for all you are
I present you with a strand of my hair,
the essence of my being,
my identity in creation.

I solemnly contemplate the
the wonders of all around me,
and know that as much as I can hear
beyond the silence
is the eternal symphony
of communicating plants.
Beyond the stillness is
the ebb and flow of energy

between every living thing.
Beyond my weakened sense of smell
are scents that of themselves are salve.
Beyond my worldly blindness
is beauty only my soul can comprehend.
My polluted taste no longer
recognises the true flavour
of what you offer me to eat.

Actions and interactions,
cycles within cycles,
hierarchies and chains.
Activity the human brain can only
understand to a limited degree.
My brain hops and bounces
at the marvel and the miracle
the magical and the mystical
and the downright incomprehensible,
all warmed by the sun,
powered by the moon,
watered by the rain,
guided by the stars.
All combined - what our spirit yearns,
the oneness of all creation
flowing from all to me
and through me to all,
and in the merging mists of time
I seek a guide to my true destiny.

15. A Perfect Day

I ran through the soft green grass
and felt the daisies between my toes,
I climbed a leafy tree
and had a look all round about me,
I paddled in the babbling brook
and tried to catch the gems
that sparkled in its water.
I gaily danced
with the waving reeds
and sang its joyful song,
as it gurgled its way
from the mountain spring
all the way to the sea.
I ambled among the gamboling lambs
as they bleated and frolicked
at the sheer delight of being alive.
I heard the gentle lowing
of the cows and the flicking of their tails
as they headed homeward
with their udders full of milk.
Then I stood ever so still,
as the shadows softly fell
on another perfect day.

16. Back To Basics

In God's masterpiece of creation
He included plants to provide
every possible constituent
needed to support and enhance
the health of the human race.
Man in his ingenuity
achieved amazing strides
in all things scientific
to provide what is widely considered
better than the equivalent
of what nature provides.
Cleanly and neatly packed
in convenient presentation,
providing apparent answers to every ill.
But along the way man strayed
from the essence of creation,
often the price to be paid
was greater than the gain.
The challenge for man today
is to assess what is the best
of our God given wealth of earth
and the best of commercial progress
so resourcefully engineered by man,
not just in relation to health,
but to environmental aspects

that make up our every day.
So every shoulder to the wheel
to wind back the clock of time
and see the miracle of plants
as God ordained their use,
supported by the wider thinking
that blends the best of progress
with what truly serves the human race.

17. Spring

Christmas shoppers,
shoulders hunched forward
against the piercing north wind,
hands thrust deep in coat pockets
and chins close to the chest
to head the biting rain,
ominous clouds portending
worse weather to come.
Though still only early afternoon
the well-lit shops are so inviting,
with their smell of coffee
and jingling bells.
But there in silence
on a bare young tree
swollen buds almost green
herald the coming of spring.

18. The Robin

The poor robin
hasn't really got a proper song,
just a rather grating tinny ticky sound.
Neither has he pretty plumes,
just dun brown feathers
and what looks like a bleeding heart.
So why for most is the cocky robin
a favourite bird
Is it because of
the way he stands on the spade
when we work in the garden
or the way he comes for crumbs
when we eat outdoors
or is it just the way he holds
his head and looks so cute
as he hops round and round,
or perhaps because we think of snowy cards
and Santa on Christmas morning?

19. The Swallow

Today I watched a swallow
flying gracefully through the air,
dipping in rhythmic flow
going hither and thither to and fro.
The slender body and delicate wings
belie the amazing strength
it takes to fly the endless miles
to find warm sunshine,
while we wrap against the cold,
then with lengthening days
back the swallow comes
to bringing another summer to our land.
What dynamo drives the tiny brain
to make the perilous trip
what intelligence makes
this little creature see
the virtue of seasonal change,
what wisdom prompts
the time to move
and when on the wing
how does this amazing
little creature get its food?

20. Gardening

When cold March winds
give way to April breezes
the garden calls for
the fork and spade
with every turn of the soil,
the energy of new growth and life
flows through the body,
bringing all the colours of the rainbow
and an overwhelming feeling
of being one with fresh green foliage,
the vibrant colours of flowers,
the spring bird song and even worms,
the warmth of the sun,
and soil brown friable and crumbly,
years of matter breaking down,
quartz, granite, slate and other stones
that could they tell stories
of where they originated,
and how they got to where they are.
how many volumes would they fill?

The heart cannot know greater joy
than when the tiny seeds are set
and all is wonder and light.
As the days grow longer
and the sun grows warmer,

like magic above the soil
appear tiny green shoots.
deeper grow the tender roots,
and with heightened anticipation
arrives the amazing experience
of the first taste
of a wide variety of vegetables,
which brought straight
from garden to kitchen table
is not just about the taste,
but the whole cycle
of connection with the earth
and the whole universe
of being sown and grown
by hand in pure organic soil.

How infuriating it is
when man decimates
the very source
of nourishment and sustenance
and aims to sate the senses
and make commercial gain
with produce that ravages the earth
and damages our health
by global mass cultivation,
artificial fertilization
and unnecessary transportation
which if not reversed,

generations yet unborn
will inherit a legacy of a barren earth
and food so far removed from what
nature intended as to be more harmful
than the intention of nourishment.

21. The Oak Tree

In our isle in a bygone age
when people were one with God and nature
unfettered by earthly trappings
the oak was the centre of ritual and celebration.
Presiding were Druids or Oak-knowers
they knew not just shape and form
but the essence of its spirit
to this day we have place names
like Cill Dara or Oakwood.

Spanning all the years
the oak has been a tree
where lovers sit beneath,
passersby seek shelter
from inclement weather,
stout branches give pleasure
to tree climbing girls and boys
and there birds build their nests
and sing sweet tunes,
on the ground beneath
the squirrels find nuts
to store for winter months.
Roots knarled and thick
burrow deep into the earth
to hold firm against the wind,
leaves rustle in the gentle breeze

and clean the air we breathe,
then in autumn they
turn to russet, amber, gold and brown
and flutter gently to the ground.
Having served for years and years,
when its day is done
it gives firewood and furniture
and so much more.

Beauty, strength and endurance
serving man and beast.

22. My Favourite Season In The Garden

If I were to name my favourite season in the garden
I just might pick the spring,
when tender green shoots
bravely break the frozen ground,
harbingers of hope and new life.
Delicate white snowdrops withstand
the fiercest winds
and daffodils dance with such joy,
filling the world with courage and light,
and bare branched trees show new seasons leaves,
that shimmer and rustle in spring sunshine.

It could be the summer,
when the roses are in bloom
and translucent leaves make dappled designs
on soft green grass,
the whole garden a perfect paradise.
So many flowers, vegetables and shrubs
all at or reaching their optimum,
all seeds sown in cooler days
arrayed in their ferny rows,
in ground still weed free,
the days are long

and the nights short and warm,
a time to breathe and reflect
between the press of spring work
and the harvesting of autumn.
Or perhaps the autumn
when the days are humid and hazy
and blooms fall and fruits and seeds ripen,
the incredulous wonder of nature,
that without prompting or educating
procures the continuity of their species,
vibrant green a short while ago
now wilting and dull,
fruit and vegetables so plump and delicious
hedges draped in vast expanses of gossamer web,
bejewelled by sparkling dew drops.

Or I might even pick the winter,
with ground shrub and tree bare,
little gardening to be done,
all so still and cold, naught about
but the spirits of souls who died down the years,
their voices heard in the howling winds
and their presence felt in the
numbing moonlit nights.
Or trees magically covered in white,
fairytale like laden branches of cypresses,
snow precariously balanced

on even the most slender branch and twig,
and a constant flurry of wings
as birds industriously feed to survive.

But then why would I pick a season,
when I can be in my garden at any time.

23. My Special Place

A sultry sun shines in a hazy August sky.
The satin soft breeze is warm and caressing
from the valley of rolling hills,
that rise mysterious and majestic
to the heather hued mountains,
with their patchwork of multi-coloured fields,
neatly sewn together with fading gorse,
and profusely populated with trees
of every species, shape and size,
many with early autumn tints,
a comforting camouflage
for the happiness, pain and struggle of life
in the shadow of their leaves.

Swallows swoop and soar,
napping unsuspecting bugs basking
on the surface of the garden pond.
The water chortles down the slate and granite stones,
to where the goldfish rest beneath watercress,
two sparrows busily feed their young
in the ivy that frames the windowpane,
chaffinches and yellowhammers chirrup
in the maple and rowan tree,
clever robin, head cocked, watches
for digging that would give him a handy snack.

Big fat pigeons perched on the cypress
give their throaty two tone coo,
the blue-tit with its high notes competes with
the thrush's varied tones,
the dog pants in the shade of the
lofty beech and apple trees,
while the young rabbits safely romp close by.
A worm invisible to the human eye, is effortlessly
flicked out from the summer lawn
by the yellow beak of the blackbird.

The geraniums, begonias, calendula and bizzy lizzies
make a blaze of reds, pinks, oranges and yellows,
the hollyhocks nod from their imperious height,
nasturtiums tumble down the rockery
scrambling over stone and plant alike,
passion flower and jasmine clamour up the pergola,
The air is filled with the heady
smell of roses and sweet pea,
freshly cut grass, rosemary, thyme,
lavender and more,
and is intensified when the dew falls
as night closes with warm still air.
In the vegetable garden the fruits of spring work
await harvesting – the pea pods
with their magic string
that when pulled opens the luscious cover to reveal

the tightly packed peas umbically
attached to alternate sides.
The potatoes that go from ground to
table and taste like no other,
beetroots, lettuce, onions and so on.
The cowslip plants proudly hold their ripe seed heads
ensuring their species for another year,
and nearby the golden sea of rippling
corn is ready for the reaper.
Silent and weightless velvet winged butterflies
flit among the echinacea, saponaria and buddleia.
While with laboured drone the
bee carries home her load
and children's laughter carries on the lazy air.

Fruit and veg, flower, tree and four legged beings,
birds, butterflies and bugs, and kids,
water, sun and breeze,
a testimony to God's boundless love and generosity,
each individual and independent,
yet part of the integral whole of creation.
All fashioned by God's hand,
not for money or fame but love.
The moment unparalleled
is the keeper of all that is gone,
And the key holder of what is to come.
A trip into the soul and separateness,
time suspended as the world goes by.

In the myriad of life, sound and movement,
there is a seamless harmony,
neither birth nor death a beginning or end,
just part of the process.
All life from the biggest tree to the tiniest insect
having its own unique value and purpose,
and as I swing gently to and fro
I know this is my special place
And no matter when, or where I am
it's where in mind's flight I can always go,
emptied of all else, to quietly contemplate
and be immersed in healing peace.
And when my mortal body is no more
my spirit will still revisit.

24. Herbal Year

The spring sunshine gently awakened
the still earth from its winter slumber,
we emerged from our hibernation,
eagerly and enthusiastically anticipating
being a part of the unfolding miracle,
our energy rising with the sap,
plants everywhere vital vibrant fresh and green
packed with every constituent
the human system could possibly need,
all just asking to show how they can
replenish renew and revitalize
all human life on earth,
the harvesting of which was guided
by lunar, solar and planetary movements.
We merged our spirits
with every precious plant we harvested
and enjoyed in return experiences
such as nettle infusion,
like a gently curving form
wafting through our bloodstream
with an expert eye noting that we needed
notching up of our metabolism
and nourishment after the depletion of winter.
Then as the summer sun rose
we celebrated our sister's maidenhood

and the promise of her feminine power and magic
which in turn celebrated the maidenhood
of us and our sisters world wide.
With midsummer we gloried in
the rich abundance basking in the warm sun
all life at its most joyful and glorious.
Autumn brought celebration of new life
the oldest and greatest miracle of creation.
As the amber leaves turned to brown
we celebrated the cronehood of our sister,
the fulfillment of life and all accumulated wisdom,
which in turn celebrated cronehood
of us and all our sisters,
and in nature we marvelled at the miracle
of seed heads and roots that ensured
the promise of plants for the coming year.
Then with shortened days and trees bared,
we gave thanks for
and celebrated our harvest of herbs
and our store of medicine
with their benefits to all mankind.
Then as the shrouding mists of November
slowly gathered
we prepared to hibernate
looking inward
at all life in suspension.

25. The Beach

Here on the beach all is mine
as I draw strength from the sea,
from its eternity, immensity,
beauty, mystery and majesty.
Here I unburden my load
and my soul keeps time
with the sea's eternal tune.
I am at one with its many moods –
now sparkling and shimmering
in the brilliant summer sun,
or whipped to a raging fury
by a relentless winter wind.
Dark and menacing -
as one with a stormy sky,
peaceful and alluring in the stillness
of the harvest moon.
Its salt on my lips
tells me I am part of
eternity and mystery
and one of the many souls she serves
and the countless spirits she stores
between her many shores.

26. On The Shore

There on the seashore
I'm in every wave that breaks
in the gulls plaintiff cry,
the soft warm sand,
and every precious gem
that sparkles in the sun.

27. The Sea

My enigmatic friend you hold me forever
enthralled and intoxicated
by your immensity, magic, mystery, ferocity,
your beauty, treachery, generosity and meanness.
On a clear day when the sun is high
you are such a beautiful,
placid, azure, sparkling blue,
an irresistible invite to
participate or just view.
But for the innocent child
or able adult alike,
should they put a foot astray,
you don't hesitate to make them pay,
while bereft family and friends
watch shocked and numbed
and try to make sense of your callous act.
When there's a cloudy sky
you are cold and green,
and can magnetise poor troubled souls
to feel being immersed in you,
will ease the black swirling in their heads.
When the moon is full
you are so alluring in
your shimmering night attire,
you still the soul and fill

to overflow all romantic beings.
When a storm brews,
and the wind howls with ferocious force,
and rain teems from a menacing dark sky,
you are a formidable and treacherous foe,
and when whipped to a furious frenzy
you heave and roll, rise, fall and crash
and relentlessly pound,
as if to decimate all.
God help the unfortunates
caught in your merciless mood,
for like matchwood you can toss and crush
even the biggest ships
and then at dawn you
can be calm and benign,
while those left behind
suffer the perpetual rerunning
of loved ones final tortuous hours,
being torn limb from limb.
But we unite in prayer
asking God to give safe passage to all
from lifeboat crew to toddler on the sand
and to gather like rosebuds those we mourn,
and grant to us left behind
the healing power of his love.

28. The Moon

The moon at its brightest
casts shadows dark and deep
when it wanes all is enveloped
in a blackness that is
hard to penetrate,
but I know when I see
that first silver sliver,
again there will be full light
even if it brings dark shadows,
just like the cycle of life.

29. A Shell

How can I be sad when I hold in my hand a shell,
for its beauty is far more than words can tell.
Yes all God's beauty is there within
the pretty pearly pattern and the whorly whirls.
How could I be lonely,
for when I put it to my ear
I can hear the echo of a distant shore,
and the endless lore in between,
of pirate ships, scary trips.
and sailors stranded on desert isles.

30. Thunderous Wave

Oh you pounding thunderous wave
that comes crashing to the shore
mindless of who we seek to save.
You come and come one time more
and each passing moment we dread
and are frightened to our very core.

We wish our friend will not be dead
but for that we need that you be still
and slumber in your sandy bed.

And that you slumber quietly until
we search and find our friend
and then our hearts with joy will fill.

And then with heartbreak at an end
we and our friend will leave you behind
and value each precious moment we spend.

But to our dying day will keep in mind
when on the shore to keep careful watch
because though beautiful you are not always kind.

When you are in a fury you have no match
And that fury can come in the twinkle of an eye
And then the unwary you easily catch.

And if there is no one on hand they die
you in uncaring mood toss them to one side
and plant in our hearts a painful sigh.

And they forever with you abide
while we depart their watery grave
and our grief we can never hide.

But then God grant that we can save
and warn others of the dangers in your water
though the pleasure of you they ever crave.

31. Energy

Ireland of the heather covered mountains
rolling hills and green fertile valleys,
where Druids walked barefoot
with utmost respect for their God
and all creation.
Then prompted by greed,
battles of man on man
grew to massacres of many
and then through ingenuity
led from crude cannons
to sophisticated bombing,
all to satisfy the greed of man
yet all the while the mountains,
rolling hills and fertile valleys,
were still as magical as ever.
But man's march went from
getting what he needed to live
in lush green forests,
to living to get what he needed
in endless concrete jungles,
with everything in his life
produced in a way far removed
from how nature intended
and has led to the ultimate
deed of greed in our history

to give financial return to a few,
some with no affinity to our isle.
Massive subsidized wind farms and attendant pylons
in the name of keeping the lights on,
but really about selling electricity
to countries who know
turbines work on free wind
but are expensive to maintain
and have a wicked carbon footprint,
leaving Ireland a graveyard
of billions of tons of cement
and disused turbines,
together with languishing children
and an epidemic of ailments.

Who are the evil perpetrators?
Not a foreign power who came with guns blazing.
No, our trusted elected
who decried their predecessors for wanton deeds.
We the people of Ireland say
No to their criminal march.

32. Space

When a loved one dies,
friends and neighbours gather round
to keep out the space their going makes.
As the people drift away
the space moves in to make all its own,
the toothbrush in its beaker,
the empty chair,
the joke to share,
the unfinished job,
the jacket just hanging there,
the laugh, the smile,
the turning key in the door –
Until then too with time the space is no more –
blended into the eternal fabric
of birth, life and death,
but forever the memories will live.

33. By Your Going

By your going you reshaped my world,
a shape I will have to learn to fit,
with a million tears and a million sighs,
a lifetime of ifs and whys,
but with a store of memories
to brighten even the darkest day.

34. Clink

Clink, clink, the manhole cover
went clink with every car that passed,
it filled the sick-room with the resonance
of the clink of prison doors.
The measured clink mingled
with the oppressive air
of the laboured breathing
and like sceptre's fingers
clutched the heart.

With the first chink of daylight
the clink was absorbed
in the bustle of a new day,
and the breathing
was of a life deceased.

35. Mortality

Your body lies still and inert,
our hearts are broken and bereft,
we miss your smile, we can't chat a while
you were always somewhere, now you're nowhere.
But more than our tear is our gripping fear,
for when you were taken our very core was shaken,
we're face to face with our mortality,
and have to review our morality.
And yet,
in a while we'll forget.
your memory we'll ever hold dear,
but mortality and morality will become less clear.

36. An Unborn

Not so long ago I was not here,
Dad and Mum had sex,
with no thought of what they had done,
nor of a daughter or son,
but here I am, unwanted by my mum
a lot of what I hear causes me to fear
I won't be here too long,
for there is a great commotion and talk of abortion.
I didn't commit a sin but I'll end up in the bin.
my mum has the right to choose,
even if Dad cares he and I will lose.
On another plane, forever hand in hand,
I'll dance in a line, with every unborn
torn from a mother's womb.

37. The Parents

These could not be the parents who begot me
when tender words of love were murmured,
these murderers who now want to abort me,
these could not be the parents who begot me
for they would welcome the product of their love,
how can their ears be so deaf and
their hearts so hard?
These could not be the parents who begot me
when tender words of love were murmured.

38. The Garden Of My Soul

In the garden of my soul
are planted all those I love and cherish,
day by day the roots go deeper
and the boughs grow stronger
and every hurt they suffer
reverberates through my being,
none more so than when one
goes to meet their maker,
then there is the wrenching of roots
and the turmoil of crashing boughs
and even when they are gone
nothing ever will be planted
in that special place,
because that is where I store
all the loving memories
of the dear departed one.

39. If I Thought

If I thought for an instant when I casually say
good-bye, good luck or cheerio,
they were my last words to you,
I would hold you, hug you and kiss you,
and tell you how much I love you.
From my heart I would pour all the emotions
of joy, pride and appreciation
of all you are and ever were.
From the bottom of my heart also
I would ask you to forgive me
anything I ever did to cause you hurt,
pain or sadness,
and I would like you to know
that though it may not always
have been your perception
everything I did was motivated by love
within the limits of my human frailty.
So now that you know,
I would ask you to cherish this cameo
and hope we have many years
before it is time for either of us to go.

40. Death

Death with its unyielding step
clutches our hearts in its icy grip
when a loved one takes that final trip,
and leaves us with a haunting echo
in the hollow of our brain,
with the eternal refrain
of why, why, why
must a loved one die?
As we look
through misty eyes at the shadow
of our former lives,
we know things
can never be the same.
Through our veins courses a searing pain,
helped only by knowing our loved one
didn't live in vain.
As we look upon
our life's shattered bits,
and feel no two fit,
we search for the reason why.
But we know the answer is on high.
for it's God's way,
and to each comes that day.

41. A Loved One

Like a green tree uprooted and turned to stick you lie.
To succour our senses we soften your starkness,
by draping you tastefully in your ultimate bed,
And repeatedly tell ourselves how restful you look,
with all care uncreased from your face,
all the while silently willing life
into your waxen remains.
Surrounded by friends and flowers,
one and all dressed in sombre colours,
we take comfort in oration,
condolences and church celebration.
Mingled with the tears we shed because you are gone
are tears for the part of us that has died.
When you are placed in the yawning hole,
and sealed away with the clammy clay,
we have to face the reality of the day.
A dark cloud shrouds our being,
wave after wave washes over us,
in a world of words we can't say how we feel –
the gnawing fear of the dark unknown,
the mystery of what is when life ceases,
the infinite emptiness and space,
the wrenching pain of the breaking chain,
the fragility of family ties, love and life,
all we thought would never change.

Images of horns, hooves and halos
of billowing clouds and white flowing robes,
screaming demons and lapping red flames.
Life, love and nature apart,
the sheer worthlessness of all.
The simple things we took for granted,
that now we'd cherish as life's treasures –
a smile, a spoken word, familiar form and foibles,
it's only with that final breath
we really know how precious was the life,
and though we wish with all our might,
we know we can never have it back.

We struggle to understand the essence of creation,
the confusion of mingled memories and reality.
All the anger, frustration, whys and wherefores,
the ifs, ands, buts and maybes.
The overwhelming guilt at leaving a loved one
alone to rot in the cold, dark, clawy clay,
while we with heavy hearts walk away.
knowing that time may heal,
but life can never ever be the same.

42. Bird Song

Every morning mingled with predawn dreams,
I hear the sweet shrill song of the birds.
As I slowly emerge from slumber,
I seek the familiar outline of my window frame
and ponder do the birds perch petrified
that light will not follow the darkness of night
and is their trill and enthusiasm
because of their daily delight?
Or is it God's design to herald
new life, new love new hope?
So I can forget yesterday's shattered dreams
and let my soul rise and shine
to be part of all that is Devine.
and thank the darkness
for taking my pain and sorrow
and the sun for bringing a new tomorrow.

43. You Are Always With Me

I turn my face to the sun,
and feel your warm embrace.
The raindrops mingle with my tears
to wash away the heartache and the yearning,
in the early morning dew drops
I see your sparkling eyes,
I feel your breath in the soft warm breeze,
and sense your smile in every living thing,
your essence wafts in the scent of flowers
and the humming of the bees.
I feel your gentle nature
in the silent flutter of butterfly wings,
your unswerving love and support
in the darkness of the night,
that always turns to light.
Your laughter echoes in the chortling water,
I hear your whispers in the rustling leaves,
murmuring gentle words of love.
In the wind I feel your strength,
and hear your voice so reassuring,
telling me one day I'll be at your side.

44. A Fly

You took a mortal blow
and fell to the ground
there you struggled and writhed
and gasped for that last breath
Then you were still.

You were but a fly.
But you were a life.

45. Our Loved Ones

Our loved ones' warm endearing smiles
beam down from heaven
enveloping us like downy soft angel wings,
protecting us from the pain of their going,
and of how things are here below.
Their thoughts like rosebuds
fill our space with love,
leaving no room for thoughts
of how it might have been.
Their home is now in heaven,
it's to there we send our love,
in our hearts we store fond memories
and pray time will heal the hurt.

46. Maura

Dear Loch Gill - serene pure waters
of the Nephin Mountains
that soothes the soul of all who come close,
my spirit lives in your ever-flowing water.
When the sun shines
I sparkle skip and sing in unison
with the tall trees the flora and fauna.
Praising and celebrating God's creation.
When the sky is grey and hangs low,
I go into my soul
and contemplate life's meaning.
When the night is dark, the rain torrential
and the wind whips the water,
I fume at man's injustice to man.
When the sun shines through the shower
my chakra colours rise to be seen from afar.
The rich red of security and support,
soft orange of pleasure and nurturing,
golden yellow of success, protection and strength,
sunlit green of peace and unconditional love,
sky-blue of acceptance of my creative nature,
indigo for the wisdom and power of my mind,
violet for my divinity and universality
and white my radiant energy.

Aura dissolving away all that is outworn,
painful and limiting,
and the white mist rising
is my spirit going to meet my God.

47. Bernie

I watch your frail and aged body
With its memory blips,
dimming eyes and diminished hearing,
strength gone from muscles once so toned and fit,
but there is a picture crystal clear of yesteryear.
lustrous hair, sparkling eyes,
skin of peaches and cream,
full of laughter and life.
The daughter who socially set the world a whirl,
the sister who made life so complete.
the beautiful bride,
beloved of a loving couple,
babies who were your pride and joy,
on whom you lavished so much love.

As they grew to maturity
imperceptibly started your demise,
to complete the cycle of a life so productive,
lived with joy, integrity and unparalleled dignity,
a gentleness recognised even by nature,
as evident by the abundant response
to your every touch.
A balance of selflessness, humility, elegance and poise
and strength second to none -
an honourable shining beacon of inspiration
to everyone whose life you touched.

48. Colleen

You dazzle us today with your brilliance,
as you shed your earthly form,
and with myriad angels
and a heavenly symphony
you go to your true home,
there at the pearly gates
to be greeted by those you love,
particularly those who love you most
- your Mum and Dad,
and then for eternity enjoy your reward,
for forty years of indescribable suffering.
Suffering borne with such strength and bravery
in the face of pain,
fortitude and courage in accepting what was,
and above all gentleness, serenity,
and dignity second to none.
On your hospital bed you asked
that we be not sad but rejoice,
for you are not going far,
and truly we can be glad,
for few of us have been touched
by someone as close as you to God.
Colleen like a glowing sunset you light our lives
and warm the darkest corners of our hearts.
no wealth, riches or fame could compare
with what you leave behind.

49. Phil

Your gentle soul has parted
from your mortal form.
Leaving us a rich legacy of
a lifetime of precious memories
of love, laughter and fun,
of someone ever young in heart and spirit,
closely tuned to the essence of being,
the meaning of life and its wisdom,
unfettered by attachment to earthly wealth.
To your last breath
you were staunchly loyal
to your values, beliefs, what you held dear
and your individuality -
as anyone who tested the waters
unquestionably discovered.
Unique is what sets us each apart,
but you Phil no words could encapsulate.
All these qualities were never more evident than
in the simple fortitude, open mindedness and dignity
with which your final illness was borne.
And Phil, as you smile down on us today,
we surrender you to God's loving care

50. I Sympathise

I sympathise with you
on your greatest loss
and know no words of mine
can ease your pain
but from what I learned
from you about your loved one
is it possible you could have heard these words......
When I have done all I can do,
paid my dues to all I owe
and lived the life God planned for me,
I will quietly close my eyes
and be happy in another place.

51. Dawn

In that sacred space as day breaks,
the moments between the darkness
of the soul searching night,
where the mind makes monsters
of thoughts and sounds,
and the turmoil of the day,
when restless minds seek
what they hope to find,
I listen to the silence
of the early morning dawn.
and stand in the wonder
of a new day not yet born.
As the world holds its breath
and the wan sun slowly
caresses the dewy earth
with its first sleepy smile,
I know in that stillness
you are there all the while.

52. What We Leave Behind

When we breathe our last
the hustle, bustle, hurry and worry
of laying up our earthly store is no more
when all our trappings are stripped away
there's naught left but what turns to clay,
yet the mark we leave behind,
are all our hopes, fears, failures,
goals and scores combined.

53. Love The Little Ones

Love the little ones,
heed their cries,
enjoy their smiles,
tarry with them a while,
listen to their prattle,
for soon they will part,
leaving you with a broken heart.
When they solemnly stand before you,
don't laugh at their attempts to grow,
for as they fumble
with life's mumbo jumbo,
they'll only be there for a day.
See the wonder of all there is,
as seen through their eyes,
and problems from their size,
for they will be gone tomorrow.
Give them hugs and kisses,
and show you love them,
for that's the essence of their existence
and the bread and butter of their being.

54. Nothing Changes

The children of yesterday
do what those before them did
and when they are dead and gone,
the same will be done
by those still in the cradle and unborn
and whether life starts
as a result of the ignominy of rape,
or a looked forward to event happily planned,
in the deprivation of extreme poverty,
or in a war torn country,
it will take its course,
and though details may differ,
and fashions come and go,
the essential essence of life
is written in stone.

55. Wealth Money Cannot Measure

When we were children we had
no labels on our clothes,
no playroom full of luxury toys,
no 100 channel silver flat screen television,
x-box, iPod or gameboy,
no hectic round of chauffeured
organised activities, parties,
outings or holidays in the sun,
when we were peckish
we had no tasty snacks,
just doorstep slices of bread and jam.
But we had wealth
money cannot measure.
The world was our oyster
limited only by the sum
of the imagination of all concerned,
we were free to come and go
pretty well as we pleased,
safe on roads, public transport
or being entertained by old men
with amazing stories to tell.

For us there were roads, dusty at times,
but virtually traffic free,

leafy bowers lined with wild flowers,
no pollution in the rivers,
no ozone layers,
nor ultra violet rays,
we romped in the sun
with no thought of cancer of the skin,
farmers' fields had no insurance fencing,
we could kick football,
with clothes for goals,
flock to rivers to swim,
skim stones, race twig boats, and fish.
watch steam engines shunt their carriages.

Summer brought haymaking,
sweet smelling grass with
daisies, buttercups and cornflowers,
which when under the scythe of the reaper
had such a special smell,
children could run hither and thither
frolicking in endless fun
up and down the winrows,
with jaunts on hay-cocks
back to the farmyard.
In the autumn there was corn to be cut,
stooked, stacked and threshed,
every available man, woman and child
gathered on farm after farm,
with all as one in hard work,

camaraderie and fun,
and meals of homemade bread and butter,
home grown cabbage and potatoes
and bacon cut from the side,
hanging in the kitchen,
pie with apples from the orchard
or blackberries from the hedgerows.
On Sundays we sensed
our elders reverence
and dutifully prayed,
we enjoyed the pomp
of wearing 'Sunday best',
the weekly roast or
chicken from a farmer's yard,
the afternoon trip to the sea,
or visits to family or friends,
all in a special air of quiet
to honour the day,
with all trade and industry ceased.
We may not have understood
but it gave us an essential pause
in which to centre our being
and start the week newly charged.

56. Rosebud

God made this rosebud
as only he alone could
in all its beauty and perfection,
just as in your every action,
His love and beauty shine through
making everything you do
a sure warm glow
that helps me know,
that I too am made by God
and am a reflection
of his beauty and perfection.
I can never thank you
for everything you do,
but I thank God each day
for putting me your way
and earnestly ask
that you may stay
forever in His love and glory

57. The Day The Pleasure Factory Broke Down

Though the sun shone
in a clear blue sky
and the birds sang
from the treetops
and the air was filled
with the smell of
lilies and roses
for me it was the day
the pleasure factory broke down,
for it was the day
my baby left home.
True my baby was twenty plus,
and God alone knows
we had our up and downs
with sleepless nights
from the earliest days
thro the teenage years,
with messy rooms
and smelly sports gear
and friends that oft
raised more than eyebrows,
good food binned
and rubbish consumed.

But all combined
each and every day
my baby was the centre
of my universe.
and truly a pleasure factory
of love laughter and emotion.

58. What A Wonderful World

In South America
in the pretty city
of La Rioja
there lives a girl
with jet black hair
and big brown eyes
and in her garden
grow amaryllis
tall elegant and
the most beautiful
shades of pink,
we imbibe
the intoxicating scent
of the evening air
while in a warm embrace
and sing from our souls
'What a wonderful World'

59. Today

We struggle with the chains of freedom
and are burdened by the power we acquire,
we are strangled by the web
of our financial transactions
and permanently stressed
by our hectic endeavours
to experience and have
all we are told life should afford us.
Our world spins so fast
we can only snatch seconds,
ever conscious that there
are a million other things
that we might or could
or should be doing.
We work for what we long for
but once got may not get the value of.
As we gorge on our greed
we are in danger of losing
sight of the ground at our feet,
and destroy the air we breathe
the land we live on
and the water that flows
in our rivers and seas.

Wistfully we run mental reels of yesteryear,
when finance, religion, society and technology

curtailed life to a slower pace but richer quality.
We can recall people who perhaps
could not read or write,
who lived the most basic lives,
yet were regal in persona,
with a comprehensive understanding
of who and what they were
and the utmost respect
for the source of their daily bread,
living so close to the earth
they could feel its very pulse,
and in their closeness to God
every moment was a prayer,
No need for them a satellite forecast,
they knew the weather's every mood,
food was fuel with thanks
offered before and after,
travel was an adventure with tales to be told,
not an irritation of constant congestion.
Calloused hands and weather beaten faces,
belied the dignity and sensitivity inside
and the deep sense of
knowingness and certainty,
of power, love and wisdom,
grown from being free of trappings.
Souls for whom the rigors of life
made simple pleasures supreme,

their most valued treasure -
the integrity of their character.

But the big wheel is turning slowly,
we now take elaborate journeys
to find our inner selves,
kit quiet rooms where we can sit,
we pay more for organic where we can,
and think a lot about what
we put into and on our bodies,
we reuse, reduce and recycle,
Green Peace row against the tide,
and Friends of the Earth guard the trees.

60. Congrats On Your Irish Citizenship

Life in Ireland in the late 1800's
Was economically dark and oppressive,
countless poor souls took the boat
to the land of promise and opportunity.
The trip was long and perilous
tossed in mountainous seas,
subjected to oppressive heat and freezing cold.
In constant contact with contagious disease,
endless hours in cramped uncomfortable conditions,
little or no food and vermin rampant at all times.
On reaching the shores of America
preservation of life was the first priority,
no welfare no hospitality no medical care,
bread and butter was the driving force.
Inch by inch a life was forged,
families formed and integrated.
with down the generations Ireland
still viewed as home
and from the financial security
of better lives grandchildren
made their way back
to a country now free of the oppressor,
economically transformed,
still green and culturally rich.

Thus Gina came back to us
with her amazing level of appreciation
and acquired folk insight,
helping us get back in touch
with the mystical elements of our life,
learning to know and use the herbs,
and make our country a better place.
So welcome and congratulations Gina
on becoming an Irish Citizen.

61. Listen

Listen to the pain behind the laughter,
feel the heartache beneath the smile,
look deep into the eyes
to see the agony some try to hide
and no matter what we have to carry,
thank God each and every day
for others have a far heavier load.

62. More Than Love

A beautiful brown-eyed girl
came through the café door she had skin like
alabaster and long chestnut hair, the clothes
she wore were trendy and chic, like a model on
the catwalk, she walked hand in hand with a
tall dark haired lad - Love's young dream? oh
so much more - for she was his eyes and ears
and only through her could he speak. With
amazing deftness tapping fingers on each
other's hands, she knew what to order
and in unspoken harmony
they enjoyed their meal.

63. Brooke - New Born

I hold you in my arms today,
tiny new born and unnamed,
you and I we span the years
from 1941 to 2006 -
four generations of mother to daughter.
Back then when someone held me in their arms,
tiny, new born and unnamed,
the guns boomed across a world at war,
sugar and tea were as gems.
Now we have a world of plenty
and may you always prosper.
But more importantly,
may you never forget
to be true to who you really are,
and remember
you are a precious link in an eternal chain
and your value is beyond measure.

64. I Love You

I love you, I love you I do
I love you with a heart that's true,
I love you, I love I do with love enough for two.
Your words forever echo in my brain,
your breath sweet and warm upon my cheek
and I'll forever hold the glow,
as we walked hand in hand down the aisle,
having vowed "til death do us part',
but when the children came along,
though they were your pride and joy,
you found other things closer to your heart,
I cried nights and ached for your arms,
now I know you'll have to go,
for they were words
and words don't butter bread,
what's done is done
and no matter what the pain,
it's your loss and my gain,
for I'm the one who stayed the course
and am stronger and wiser,
than when you used to say,
I love you, I love you I do
I love you with a heart that's true
I love you, I love you I do with love enough for two.

65. The Ruined Abbey

I sit by the ancient ruined Abbey,
with its beautiful cut red-sandstone
and granite portals and window frames,
I melt away the modern buildings,
paving and the traffic,
leaving the blue cotton ball clouded sky
and the honey hued sun dappling every surface,
as it shines through spring leaved birch trees.
On the street the dust comes through the toes
of barefoot children dressed in rough homespun
woollen and linen clothes and homely hairstyles.
Smoke curls from the small mud
walled thatched houses,
where women in full skirts with arms thick from work,
cook, spin, wash and tend animals
with toddlers in tow.
Inside the Abbey are smells of bees wax,
timber browned with age and burning candles.
The chanting voices of the monks
rise in harmonious praise of God,
their hands rough and knarled from
the manual work of self-sufficiency.
Horns blow in traffic jam rage
cruelly bringing me back
to the present and chaos.

66. To The Newlweds

May you both have a lifetime
of love, health and happiness,
with neither one leading nor following,
but both walking hand in hand,
each with a shoulder to the load
and a shoulder for each other to lean on,
looking deep into the eyes of each other,
ever seeking to know what it takes
to make that vital connection
and a marriage that works,
not just for you both
but for the precious
beings you are blessed with.

67. My Soulmate

My soul mate listens to
my deepest worries and concerns,
to my darkest secrets,
greatest joys and triumphs,
dearest dreams and ambitions,
and never judges or condemns.

My beloved friend
never hurts or offends me,
never demands or rejects,
always puts me first
and strives to give me
everything I want or need.

My love respects all I do,
surprises me with romantic gestures,
makes me feel so special,
is my soft place to fall,
a shoulder to cry on,
a helping hand when needed.

All of this I try to mirror,
so like two candles with one flame,
two spirits merged as one,
we have total connection,
all issues based on each other,
and the common good of both.

We laugh and cry together,
and never ever let the
sun go down on our anger,
or leave issues unresolved,
For nothing is more precious
Than the love we two share.

68. Elvis

During the ebbing years of war,
in the land of promise and free speech,
the world was sent reeling
by the electric surge of pop,
headed by Elvis the
undisputed king of rock,
who unleashed an audacious
and outrageous style
in music dress and
gyrating body movements,
causing his fans to scream with delight
and grannies to shield younger eyes.
The king revelled in
his undreamed of wealth and glory,
but sadly his fame
was bigger than his stature
and like a candle snuffed out
one day he was suddenly gone,
leaving us his wealth
of music and memorabilia.

69. Life In An Instant

If for an instant you've ever looked
deep into a stranger's eyes
and there seen all your heart desired
and felt both your souls unite,
even if you never ever meet again
you know in that moment
your world was perfect and complete.

70. The Fire

On a cold winter's night
in a room otherwise unlit
you are a creative flicker
and a memory tracer,
a shadow movie-maker,
a once-upon-a-time store raker
and with your last embers,
a sound night sleep maker.

71. Your First Babygro

I hold your very first babygro to my face
and can easily recall your special baby smell
and everything that was you
and as if it was now I hear you chortle and coo

I feel your pain when you cried,
I bask in the brilliance of your smile,
your laughter ripples through my veins
to bubble in my heart

I feel the softness of your hand
as you explore my face,
the joy and pleasure of your every stage,
first words, first steps and all the firsts

Your school your friends sport and all that,
the teenage years and your first loves,
now that you are an adult of the world
I walk with you every step

I see your face in your mirror
as you prepare for another day
I see you through the eyes of others
in a world the better for having you

I feel your energy clear and vibrant,
with all the colours of the rainbow

and hear your voice unique to you,
as you greet all you meet

With love and care I'll put away
your very first babygro
and as I go on my daily round
I'll cherish every precious memory.

72. Angel Rod

Some fish in troubled minds
of hurt and shattered dreams
seeking the rays that will
light new tomorrows,
may the Angel Rod
be symbolic of Angelic guidance
in their daily quest.

73. Free

In the boundless world of my mind
I skim across green meadows,
and run to meet rolling waves.
At night I dance barefoot to magic music,
and sing with Pavarotti.
I climb the tallest mountain,
and ride the high sea.
I laugh and joke like other folk,
I feel the chill wind, and the warm sun,
and know very well I'm a man,
you can ask *me* do I take sugar,
I can tell you I have pain,
but my life is not in vain,
for though I'm wheelchair bound,
in my heart and head all emotions abound.

74. You Have An Angel

You have your own very special angel
always and ever with you
every waking and sleeping moment of the day,
every step you take and every word you speak
every breath you breathe,
someone who knows your every
thought hurt and hope
and if you open wide your heart
and treasure this precious presence,
life's dips will be lightened
and pleasures and joys heightened

75. Time

Time - the merciless master
who looks at us askance
as we flit across his palm
he treats us with indifference
as we struggle with our insignificance
in relation to the magnificence
of his overall plan,
while the mountains that touch the sky
and the oceans wide are safe in his keep.

76. A Moment

A moment snatched,
poignant and still,
in a life of strife,
to give a lifetime
of loving memories.

77. Life

We start as a drop in the ocean of life.
and make our way to the shore,
we wax and grow in our joy and woe.
And if things go right
we arrive at our height,
to briefly kiss the shore
and then go to be no more.

78. Reality

Like a shaft of light
on a dark night
sometimes we can suddenly see
that *that* which we thought was *was* not
and that which we never imagined
was in reality the fact.

79. Radio Éireann

My bouffant hair style was lacquered
to the point of cracking,
bees all but physically present
I stepped through the Henry Street door of the GPO,
into the building that housed Radio Eireann,
with all the confidence and experience
of my nineteen years and leaving the lift,
I casually acknowledged the porter.
The deep piled carpet robbed my stiletto heels
of their staccato sound.
With the arrogance and ignorance of youth
I had no mind to the historical wealth
of the building I daily frequented.

80. Illusions

Just as colours are but an illusion
caused by the sun's collusion,
all that we think hope, feel and see,
is not really what it appears to be,
but rather an illusion,
caused by life's confusion,
so too what we seek we may not find,
like the rainbow end.

81. A Thought

A thought is a seed
sown in the brain,
fed by experience
of love, joy or pain.
watered by our nature
and reaped in a time
of quiet contemplation,
or sometimes it can flit
before we have time to register it.

82. Love

What a tangled web is woven of love, hate and need.
the silken threads of lives ever crossing,
yet always separate
not loving any less,
just never knowing,
that it is not what the giver wants to give,
but the receiver's need,
that makes happiness.

83. Sunbeam

Hope springs eternal
my little sunbeam,
that comes with every ray,
to brighten my day,
will it forever dance way out there,
or someday will it blind me with its brilliance,
as it fills the space all round me?

84. Questions

Questions, questions, questions,
answers follow questions,
questions beg answers,
the more you wish to know,
the more questions there are.
All answers have questions,
not all questions have answers.

85. Poor Old Teddy

I sat and sewed a teddy today,
so what you may well say
and indeed to look at the poor dear
you'd be right to fear
he's for the high jump,
yes off to the dump,
for he can neither hear nor see
his mouth is not where it used to be,
his coat is all bald and bare,
with holes here and there.
But on the sunny summer morn,
when our little girl was born,
he was all plump, soft and fluffy
and the colour of creamy coffee.
His big brown eyes
were full of surprise
and from that date
he became her constant mate
and though he got many a thump
and from the pram many a bump
and was carried without fail every day
in a most incongruous way,
it was in him she would confide,
for she always knew he was on her side,
it was he who dried her tears

and chased away her fears,
At night when she'd be asleep,
I'd often go and peep
and there in blissful repose
the two would be cuddled close.
To me looking back the most serious lack
in the life of our daughter,
would not have been a mother or father,
but this now decrepit expression
of her most treasured friend and possession.

86. *Lyons Tea Tokens*

When I was a very young bride
I looked after my husband with utmost pride,
that was plain for all to see
because I always served him Lyons tea
and then there was for me the Merry Minstrels,
those lilting toe tapping *tripsters*
who held the key to my ultimate dream,
through ever so simple a scheme,
yes, one day I would drive near and far
in my longed for prize of a car,
so with dedication and hopeful emotion,
I persistently collected the 40 objects of my devotion,
but with the passing of the years
I was assailed by ever increasing fears,
that all those beautiful cars
were ending up on Mars,
for I never saw nor heard of one,
in spite of all the slogans I had done.
But now I am told in my stars
my name must be on one of those cars.

87. The Old Woman

There was an old woman of dubious renown
who always wore a frown
her dog killed her cat
the old woman said 'that's that'
and with a very cross face
flew into outer space
there she got hit by a rock
it was such a hard knock
she dropped nice as could be
with a splash into the sea.

88. Limerick
(Gay Byrne Show)

There was a young turkey called Gaybo,
who dreaded the annual hey-ho,
but he just sat tight
and prayed every night
that he'd become an elderly Gaybo.

89. Student

Your black head bent
tired brain taut
energy taken from the sun and moon,
eye on independence soon,
all those hours of learning
in tune with your hearts yearning,
no more figuring where to get a fiver,
or counting the cost of a crust.
May success walk step for step with you,
and lady luck smile on everything you do,
and may you yet manage to stay true,
if life cuts short your dream
and your bubble bursts before you've been,
remember you're still you
and may you find the happiness that's yours
in everything you do.

90. Eternity

I look into the eternity of the sky
as it spans my world,
so too it did that of my ancestors and theirs
for all the years.
I look at the thunderous wave,
that crashes on the rocky shore
and then comes once more
again and again for ever more,
or the sun that rises and shines
and then is gone,
to rise and rise for all time
and for an instant I am.

91. Thank You Granny

I still remember you sitting there,
in your black silky clothes and grey hair,
when I'd have a broken heart
you'd take me on your lap,
nestle my head to your breast,
to rise and fall to the gentle rhythm of your breath,
you'd wipe away my tears,
smooth my tousled hair,
and hush my cries with soothing sounds.
When you'd find the smile I tried to hide,
I'd run away and play,
with no thought to say 'Thank you'
and this I say today.

92. Women

We send men to the moon
and talk on a video phone
but women still live in shades of a darker age
women are more free to have a job
but compared with men their pay is a rob
and men are still more free for golf or the pub
today's man can toss a crepe and change a nappy,
but when it comes to dodging child-rearing,
he is still more snappy,
while there are exceptions to every rule,
to be a man is still more cool.

93. The Auction

'Auction' arrows and lines of parked cars
mark the house for 'Sale',
with expectant step people make their way,
the hallway muddied by the feet of vultures,
coming to pick the bones of the dead home.
With narrowed eyes every inch is scrutinized.
The defenceless walls denuded of their chattels,
unable to conceal the faded paper
and scuffed paintwork.
The little glass lady dismissed as crass,
unable to shout out that she was bought
by a small boy who spent every penny he had
on his first school tour because he wanted to show
how much he loved his mum and dad.
The heart has ceased to beat,
the house is but bricks and mortar,
no one hears the haunting echo
of children's laughter, play and chatter,
birthday and Christmas celebrations,
The pain of birth and agony of death.
Soulless they pick and prod and go their way
with their bargain of the day.

94. Sheila Wingfield

Her porcelain beauty belied the pain
of the turbulence within,
at once compliant yet ever rebelling,
a state created by a shattered world at war,
money and status that mocked her free spirit,
a religion that ball and chained her
and loving parents that ripped her apart,
in an unsettled life of constant contrast
was she hiding or was she chasing?
Was it pain made her seek refuge
in Greek mythology?
Or was it there she found the magic
that made her as radiant
as crystal that needs the sun
to reveal its brilliant colours?
Was the pen the unfettering key
or the sword to fight?
Did literature flow from her emotional well,
or did it fill the vacuum?
Was her yearning for the earthy
a desire for nature?
Or repulsion for the pain of her ultimate social gaffe?
Was the social moulding the cement that held
or literature the valve?
When she lay in bed at night,

her soft skin caressed by fresh satin sheets,
lovingly turned down by her faithful maid,
fuelled by what she imbibed,
what fantasies did she play out
on the high ornate ceiling of her privileged home,
as her beloved children slept in another room,
innocent of being deprived?
And if we were privy to her uncensored thoughts,
to what heights or depths would we be plunged?
In her autumn years
did she tame the forces within
by resorting to illusion of what was or was not?
Or was it that she so lost it that
she simply didn't know
reality from illusion?
From her simple grave in Clara
she can smile on our perplexities,
for she alone knows.
If in fact even she ever knew.

95. Youth

The lost years of careless youth
purse strings opened and spent with abandon,
ignorance and arrogance preventing realization
of the value of the greatest assets we could possess
– youth and time.
We strove to mark ourselves apart
from our staid plodding forbears,
with their bill paying money saving complex,
we pushed to experience life at the limit,
ignoring pleas for caution and temperance,
not for us the mediocrity of nine to five,
early to bed and early to rise,
just night long beer, take away, loud
music and what have you,
followed by daylight hours under the duvet.
Earn money – nah.
The hole in the wall was *yer* only way.
Until like Dracula one day,
we saw the light
and the people we were took flight.

96. Be Free Of Fear

Every human of basic reasoning
has an unquestionable right
at every point of life to make a choice
even if that choice be to do or die.
Unfortunately for the human race
all down the ages,
this ever so precious gift
has been governed by fear.
Fear the greatest human weakness
that has dammed generations
into unthinking slavery of thought.
Condemning countless souls
to a shackled life lived in fear of
being a success or a failure,
of doing or not doing,
fear of what people might say,
or how they might not understand,
or what might be expected or not accepted,
by elders, parents, peers or employers.
Perhaps our greatest fears
are those around us facing
the demons that damn us,
by keeping us from
being who we might be,

because we cannot take the step
from where we are
to where we could be

But when all is said and done
and to be totally liberated
the only thing we need to fear is fear.

97. Wexford

Oh my beloved Wexford, whose dear heart
proudly beats between the majestic
Blackstair Mountains
and the sea that laps at the south-eastern shore.
In your bosom you have nurtured
centuries of Wexfordians, proud to carry the name,
many immortalised in the annals of the world.
Foes came to pillage, but fell in love with you,
and you became their motherland.
Others came with black hearts and greedy eyes,
and you spent three hundred
years listening to the cries
of your children being stripped of
all they had or ever could be,
not for them to own house, horse or land,
exercise their vote, or have a skill,
they even had to speak with a foreign tongue,
and cease to worship their God,
all achieved with the help of the pitch
cap, rack, bayonet and torch,
leaving nothing but to be subservient
to the tyrannical foe.

Until one day when they were bowed
as far as they could go,

no more feeling of pain, and no
more tears left to shed,
they sensed your pulse and turned to challenge
the military might of the oppressive tyrant,
then the summer air was filled with war cries
and the clash of bayonet on crude pike,
the hovels that were homes were
burned to the ground,
women and children cowered in the hedgerow,
waiting for the mortal blow.
It was no surprise they lost the fight,
but it sowed the seed that in years to come
would give a rich harvest.

You were never more resplendent than now
in your beauty and bounty,
your richly wooded hills and valleys,
your rivers, mountains and golden sands,
all so favoured by the sun
and your children flourish in
undreamed of prosperity,
their love for you intensified by
oppression and deprivation,
the names of those who travelled afar
and achieved the highest honours in other lands,
echo mingling with those of your
heroic sons and daughters,
who never left their beloved land.

98. Peace

Peace comes slowly
like the sun over the hill,
lighting our lives with the love of our foes.
For all the years
that we yearned we all learned
how to hold our heads,
and smile through the tears
of our hurts and fears.
Now we know to let this love grow
we must be gentle tolerant and kind,
for there's a new tomorrow
there for us to find.

99. 1798

The Celtic tiger has been,
everywhere his good can be seen,
we've never had such prosperity in this land
and the wealth is in the Irish hand
but we might not be in this happy state
if it were not for the rising of 1798.

Our pastures are lush and fruitful
and harvests generous and bountiful,
not but that this was always a green land,
just the wealth was in a foreign hand.
Now every hour's labour
is for our kith and kin and neighbour,
no more for us a people cowed,
with heads lowly bowed
and hearts so full of hurt and hate,
thanks to the rising of 1798.
No more for us a defenseless folk
burdened with a senseless yoke,
now a people with heads held high,
knowing we no longer have to die
to own a home to vote or learn to read or write
thanks to the rising of 1798.

100. Conflict

In this little isle of ours people daily
use so much power to cause
unspeakable pain as they kill and maim,
which is all so totally pointless, for
while great men stand on their might,
completely committed to the fight,
tomorrow's unborn child
has died before it has cried,
to have any hope of peace
all of this has to cease,
but while we wait for it to stop
sombre suits talk at the top,
endlessly discussing the atrocities
and others suffer the complexities
of yesterday's political folly,
not knowing who is foe or ally,
no platitudes can justify the cost
of the legions of lives lost,
because of being on one's side
of the religious or political divide,
living life in the shadow of the gun,
innocent of the wrong that was done.
Why can't we all look at one another?
and see only a sister or brother,
for we all talk to the same God

and eat from the same sod,
we all breathe the same air,
and need the same care,
to deal with daily strife,
what really matters is life,
for each that delicate thread
that hangs between living and dead,
a thread that causes such dread
when broken because God has spoken,
but becomes an unspeakable deed,
when it happens because of land or creed.
So let's all join in a prayer
that everyone may share
this land we dearly love,
knowing it belongs to God above
and that nothing can ever be won
by force, the bomb or gun.

101. Good Friday 1998

Peace is on hand for the people of this land,
ghosts of the past can be laid to rest at last,
on Good Friday Christ died
now we Irish can look on it with more pride,
the day of the Good Friday Agreement,
a step to the end of Kathleen's Lament
from 1798 to 1998
was a long time to wait
for a healing of ancient sores,
but now peace comes to our shores,
a peace that was won
without the use of bomb or gun,
a peace to immortalize
Gerry Adams, John Hume
Bertie Ahern, David Andrews
Tony Blair, Mo Mowlam,
David Trimble
And many more.
Yes history in the making
and Peace for the taking.

102. Enough Is Enough

In the year nineteen sixteen
good women and men
like their forefathers,
gave their lives and their all,
to free Ireland from the foreign foe
from centuries of tyranny
that left the nation bereft of all,
downtrodden destitute illiterate,
denied all but their spirit.
That spirit fired their ingenuity
that made up for no resources
and so with pen and pike,
dressed in peasant gear,
they faced the fearsome foe
royally arrayed in army attire,
their losses were beyond
basic human comprehension,
but their determination for freedom
spurred their darkest moments,
like insects undercover
no gathering of groups allowed,
they communicated by nod and wink
and a runner where they could.

And so just when they thought
it was all for naught,

that light at the end of the tunnel
grew brighter and brighter
until the wildest dreams
of countless generations,
were there for the taking
and so from the depts
they built a nation free,
that forever would bear scars.
Peace and prosperity for all
motivated their every thought,
the sun shone and the rain blessed
the fertile green isle,
people grew and prospered
until those in government
were powered by the pound,
which went from bad to worse
and ended in financial ruin,
followed by the ultimate deed of greed
developer led turbines littering the land
with their partners the pylons
dominating the hard won land.

Who took everything
and denied the Irish all rights

103. The Celtic Tiger

In a troubled country financially skint,
people were beleaguered by few jobs and low pay,
then on the doorstep was the Celtic cub,
when economic clouds hung dark and low.

The cub was all cuddly and cute
emitting a message to one and all,
here's the answer to our problems
for times are very tough.

Slowly people took the bait
with no great expectation
but then the economic tide turned
and the cub began to growl.

With sights set high for good living,
soon the dark days were in the past,
until economists murmured warnings,
and rumbles echoed throughout the land.

Living privilege and luxury undreamed of
heads were turned and hearts grew proud.
But the bigger the tiger grew
the more it growled and growled.

It growled here and sniffed there,
and caused more and more unease
and many began to read between the lines
and back out of the Celtic Tiger league.

A plague on that cuddly cub
thought one and all as the frenzy rose,
it has to be stopped
before we are all destroyed.

Then there followed financial chaos
as the net closed on one and all,
the Celtic tiger crouched
and economic clouds hung dark and low.

The celtic tiger turned and slinked
with disgruntled growls
sending the message to be rich or poor
times are tough.

The chaos like a frenzied storm
round and round the country raged,
until every house felt
the quivers and feared what next.
Like there was no end,
each day brought further wrath,
until it did appear
the country was a shambles.

While those who could,
dodged the worst of the mire,
the country as a whole gladly said
goodbye to the Celtic Tiger.

104. Life Is Like A Maze

Life is like a massive maze,
solid walls around every corner
and in life and maze alike,
the key to happiness
is not to try to go up and over,
down and under around or through,
but to pick a path of peace
that will lead you to where
you rightfully should be.

105. For-Get-Me-Nots

If it were summer
and forget-me-nots graced my garden
I would pick them for you.
not that you might remember me,
but to say I will never forget
your kindness, generosity and compassion
in opening doors to set me free.
Sadly forget-me-nots
are bound in the chill winter earth
awaiting warm sunshine and gentle rain
to restore them to their glory.

106. Thoughts

Myriad thoughts come
crashing, crushing and crowding,
like the waves on the rocky shore,
relentlessly pounding and rushing,
only to mix and ebb and be no more,
just like the endless ocean,
blending with the menacing sky,
housing the infinite thoughts,
hurts, pains and doubts,
ever the same,
yet ever changing.
At dawn and dusk
sky and sea are as one,
and belie all the turmoil
by being so peaceful and still.

107. Our Friend
– Our Breath

The worst place ever to be
is in the endless corridors of the mind
when troubled thoughts
go on the rampage,
crashing and careering about,
opening countless doors,
to let millions of other contentious
thoughts join the fray
of fear hurt and anger.
Rhyme and reason
cower in dark corners
unable to compete,
chaos reigns supreme,
until we remember our friend –
our breath,
then together we slowly draw in peace
to every fibre of our being,
and expel all troubled thoughts,
restoring calm and centeredness.

Like a ribbon of white misty fog
that in Autumn hovers
just above the fields and hedgerows,
peace wafts through our toes,

it twirls up our legs,
filling our tummy and ribcage,
then from our fingers
up to our shoulders,
curling through our throat
to swirl around in our head,
then ever so slowly,
we let out that white ribbon of peace
and around our body it spirals,
from the top of our head to our toes,
to envelop us in soft white peace.

108. Silence

A prison is not just bricks and bars,
but what we build in our heart
to keep all out and us within
and there we pine,
for what we have not
and what God has not given.
Each brick is the hurt
we see in what others do and say,
cemented with the anger we display.
When it started maybe we cannot not tell,
indeed there may be no memory at all,
but bit-by-bit we built
a step and one step more,
until we were secure,
as behind any prison door.
No machine can knock these walls,
nor warden hear our calls.
What we need is quietness.
Not the empty silence of the absence of noise,
but the full quietness
of the presence of God.
This is ours for the asking,
it can't be got by might,
but by emptying our soul and mind
at the feet of the maker of mankind.

109. Embrace The Child Within

There on the swinging garden seat
sat the five and sixty-three year old
the years of silence loomed large between them
eyes forward contemplating the pond.
The voice of the sixty-three year old said
'a funny world those fish live in,
they never come out to stand or talk',
the five-year old leaned forward,
the better to examine their plight,
then turning and with all the wisdom
and clarity of her years said
'but they play hide and seek all day,
and never have to wonder where grown-ups go
or if they will come back,
or worry what tomorrow will bring'.
The freckled face framed with dark plaits,
was serious, the sombre hazel eyes,
went beyond the triviality of the remark.
The lump in the sixty-three year old throat
was not so much for what happened,
as how little could be done to ease the pain.
With eyes locked their hands touched,
slowly and when both were ready they hugged,
the tears flowed the years melted away
and the sixty-three and five year old were one.

110. Wonky Boat

I put to sea in a wonky boat,
the sails were torn and the rudder worn,
but I steered a steady course,
and thought I was doing quite well,
until one day I said to hell,
I'll put these things to right,
so I worked day and night,
but all to no avail,
now I sit and drift,
because I have neither sail nor rudder,
and can neither,
make it there nor back,
and at dawn when the sea will be calm,
and the wan sun slowly warming,
I will just close my eyes
and let my spirit rise,
and I will be free.

111. Stubble Field

Brown, bare and stark, savagely
stripped of all you bore, sorely hurting,
defenseless against the numbing frost and
teeming rains, poor picking for birds
desperate to maintain winter weight.
Throwing up for us bones picked
clean of flesh as spirits restless in
the hoary moonlight strive to reconnect
with a life-long left behind,
stubby bristles warding off
any gentle approach.
While the ploughman with toasty toes,
light head and notched out belt is
mindless of the enormity
of your contribution
to his daily stead,
too busy with the hectic round,
immersed in sparkling seasonality,
until you with a weary sigh,
succumb under a blanket of snow,
waiting for the call when he emerges with
green shoots and glistening steel
confident that once again
you will indulge his need.

112. Life

When life deals a hand that hurts
and shatters our fragile psyche
we grow strong in broken places,
as we strive to build a life that works for us,
we may rise and shine like a meteor in flight,
or be locked in a living hell of hurt and guilt.
The cracks in our construct
can let the world extend the spiral
to carry even beyond our grave,
until if we are lucky somehow we get a tap
that opens doors to set us free
to live a sweeter life.
Enhanced by life's challenge
with a new song in our heart,
feet stepping to a lighter tune and going forward,
we drink in that sun rising on our new horizon
and watch it sparkle and shimmer on our sea of life.

113. The Cry Of The Quadriphlegic

In the endless hours of the night
when neither the sun nor moon shed their light,
I search the dark silent corners of my soul
and with a soundless scream,
I beg God to let me know
why he burdens me so with these useless limbs,
confining me in tortuous corridors to writhe in pain
and live a life that seems so in vain,
so robbed of the basic joy
of what others count as mundane.
But then with the first creep of dawn
and the early chorus of birdsong,
His answer comes clear and strong
and though I know my load will not be lightened,
my awareness of the essence of life is heightened
and I know if only I can be still and accept his will,
that the good God above
will tenderly wrap me in His love.

114. Perfection

We are born perfect mirror images
of the God of our creation
complete with infinite creative potential,
the presence of which is evident
from the reaction of all ages
to the wonder of a new born.

Our eyes are capable of absorbing the world wide,
our laughter is of unadulterated love, joy, and mirth,
accepting and trusting of what life has to offer,
even to death like Icarus.
We come with 360° vision of life,
which is reduced to a tunnel view,
by the mould we are shaped to,
leaving us like aged unopened rosebuds.

Even before we arrive
the world that welcomes us with open arms
has ready the mould to sustain
the essence of our being,
- a frame to enable order and moral integrity.
From the pink and blue that says 'that's you',
to the who our parents talk to,
and the money bracket they're in,
and the colour of their skin,
the protocol written by souls long gone

and the echo of distant battles lost and won
by a native or foreign king

As our innocence ebbs
we learn to shape our own mould.
Niggly whisperings in our head
are soon quelled
with 'I must, I mustn't I should,
I shouldn't, it's not for me'.
All the while our physical form develops
to the delight of one and all
and belies the turmoil it hides
in the essence of our being,
until with time the mould is complete.
We grope through
the darkness of our half-life
and live to the level of our limitations
a never ending war,
with more battles lost than won,
ever more oblivious of the core within,
but managing as with a damaged limb.
When the troubles rain
from the clouds we create
they sear our senses and cause us pain.

Many die never knowing
the how or why,
some know but never understand,

others are lucky and spot
a star whose path
leads them to a higher plane
and though it's steep it's worth the pain.
But like the climber pressed
against the mountain face
to look ahead is too daunting,
and to look back is heartbreak,
all that was familiar is left behind,
the only option is to
focus on one step at a time,
to get to the goal and the ultimate prize
– the unshakeable serenity
of higher self,
and a life to be lived
as it was meant to be,
and because we
grow strong in broken places
life is more sweet and dearer,
and has dimensions it might never have
if our path had not diverged.
from this elevated position.
Life is seen in perspective,
all that was menacing,
hurtful, longed for or important
becomes so irrelevant,
and the state of being, just breathing,

becomes the most important state,
all else falling away,
and God is so close
there is no need to pray,
for He is in every breath we breathe.

115. My Soul

Be still my soul and let God's love wash o'er
then to your heavenly home you can soar,
forever to dwell above in God's eternal love,
far from your earthly life with its struggle and strife.

116. Me

Of all the people in my life
I'm the hardest one to get to know
yes I'm aware of the colour of my hair,
now more than speckled grey,
my eyes are green and have lost
the sparkle of youth,
I'm five feet two inches tall
and most important - a quarter,
I know what I love to eat
and would never touch,
what makes me glad or sad,
the things I love to do
and everything I hate.

But the one thing I'll never know
is how others see me
and what they really think of me.

117. Seashore

There on the long seashore
there is magic and mystery to explore,
to know God above made the sand, sky and sea
and see his beauty in all three,
uncluttered by house or office block,
articulated truck or clock.
To be at one with nature
and sense the immensity
and endless eternity
of that water that flows from shore to shore,
with its golden edge of sand,
to know how many souls
it touches that yearn to be free,
free of life's struggle and strife,
hurt, pain and confusions
and endless shattered illusions.

118. Feelings

Oh feelings how you flit and duck and hide,
be still,
that I may know you better.
You are like a sunbeam that I can see
but just cannot ever touch,
or like the martin who spends
a lifetime on the wing,
who swoops and soars,
but only ever lets you see
his outline against the sky
and if I cannot know my feelings
how can I know me?

119. Walk

I don't want to stay,
to fight another day,
I am tired and weary,
lost, confused and dreary,
and would like to take a walk
from the sea shore
to way out there
to walk and walk,
and not think or talk,
or feel what's right or wrong,
or worry about what's to be done,
but let the soft warm comforting sea,
wash over and cradle me,
in its infinite bosom,
and gently waft me to and fro,
that I might let my burden drift and flow.

120. Sea Of Life

Out here on the bleak soul searching sea of life I ride,
it is as if every demon has been released on me,
as the raging tumultuous torrents
of the merciless mountainous sea
takes its anger out on me,
the seething surf churns my guts,
the dark menacing sky presses
down and smothers me,
the million angry voices
of the relentless searing wind
scream in my soul,
and choke the breath in me,
and try to tear me apart,
while a million arrows rain on my numbed frame,
seeking the very marrow of my bone,
and oh I am so alone,
and think how nice it would be
to be in a calm sunny sea.

121. Shells

These shells once pretty and golden
that graced the floor of the ocean
were born in the eye of a storm
and tossed in a raging torrent
then carried in seething surf
and brought together
by a fearful current
to be bonded that no might could part
they were browned in the murky depts
and yellowed with years of fear
and now lie scarred
by all their hurts.

122. Change The Tune

Slow and tortuous like the tortoise,
my heart and head so low
it was difficult for me to know
which way to go,
I worried, fretted and gathered
others' pains and woes
and gave to many the power to hurt,
until getting slower and slower one day
my body said stop,
and then from where I'll never know
came an angel's spark,
and shot through the fog
that was my brain,
it lit my way
to one who turned me round again,
'drop your load' I was told,
'and have some fun'.

The *how* troubled my befuddled head.
more difficult it was to me
than a tortoise trying to dance,
for my load was more than part of me,
growing as long as my memory,
tears of weariness and frustration flowed,
confusion reigned and there I thought I'd never get.
Much harder than learning the new

was unlearning the old.
But again the angel that someone sent,
chipped a chink and let me see
a world of wonder
as yet unknown to me,
little by little I raised my head
and saw the signs that were always there,
so plain and easy to understand.

First I had to feel free to love me,
and see my God given gifts and beauty,
and joy and beauty everywhere,
to forgive myself for all I thought I did or didn't do,
and others too - to heal the hurts of all the years,
To play hide and seek
with the child I left behind,
and know I don't need to be so strong,
to peek into every nook and corner
and see every petal on every flower,
to be the me I never knew,
and know that the thought I hold will hold my day,
and the goal I set will shape my future,
to still my mind and live the moment,
and to know that to be happy
I must let the little seed grow,
to do what I do because my heart wants to
and not let the need to win rob my power,
to remember that the sparrows

and the lilies do not reap or sow,
and that when I knock it will be opened to me,
to realize that good or bad
every experience is my building block of happiness,
and that all in all I am so blessed.

Now when hurt threatens I enfold myself in love
and deflect the pain with positive thoughts,
and from my elevated position
disasters just melt away,
now I can reach my door to the universe
and bathe in its eternal light.
and stripped of all the layers I thought was me,
there shines a jewel so bright,
so that now I know my barriers,
like childhood bogeymen will float away,
and I also know that I alone
am the architect and keeper
of my every thought and deed,
hope, aspiration, hurt and fear.
Equipped with this simple knowledge
my everyday is coloured a brighter hue,
and within I can build a whole new me.
Like the boat though beautiful in the bay
must sail the sea for that's where it was made to be.

123. A Life Examined

I have travelled my longest life journey,
starting in a fog of confusion,
then scaling my highest mountain,
to view my vast potential,
down into the deepest ravine,
with the dawning of realization
of where I have been,
a turbulent trip on a stormy ocean,
when feelings and emotions emerged,
requiring excruciating twists and turns
as I strove to unlearn and learn.
my darkest moment when I saw what was required,
my brightest when I saw my way
by negotiating myriad cross roads
and reading endless signposts,
to arrive at a vision of my astounding oasis,
a place of serenity, abundance and power,
to be nurtured and developed until my dying day.

124. When We Are Dealt A Hand That Hurts

When we are dealt a hand that hurts
shattering our fragile psyche,
we grow strong in broken places
and build a life that works for us
based on a cycle of fear, hurt and guilt.
The cracks in our construct
can let the world extend the spiral
to carry even beyond our grave,
unless perchance our guiding spirit
steers our step to cross the path
of those with vision and compassion,
then skilfully the layers are peeled
to reveal to us the brilliance
of the most simple facts
in balancing life's inequities.
No words can express gratitude
for empowering us to redress issues
and may they long continue
to use their expertise
in enabling others to benefit.

125. I Am The Mother

I am the mother of those children
because for nine months I carried them
and marvelled at the miracle
of their human perfection
when first they were born.
I am the mother of those children
for I tended and cared for them
daily in their every need
and regularly walked the floor
in the long hours of the night.
My heart jumped for joy
when they were happy
and broke when they were sad
I was there for all their firsts and lasts
to cheer and wipe the tears
and urge them to do what was
in the best interest of their welfare
I taught them all I knew
to make it in this life.

Or am I the child?
for it is they who
taught me there is no pain in sacrifice
when it is for the one you love,
and there is no greater love
than that of a mother for her child.

It is they who taught me
there is no greater gift
than the uninhibited look smile or hug,
that only a mother can get from her child.
Through their eyes I saw what
I missed through doubts and fearful choices.
Then as they matured
they opened doors and raised the bar,
leading me to do things,
that perhaps but for them,
I would never have thought to do,
then it was their time to know
what was best for me.
So am I the mother or the child?

126. Ireland

Ireland of the rolling hills mountains
and fertile valleys,
where Druids trod barefoot
in tune with nature, the universe
and the maker of all they knew.
Their food and clothes and all they needed
to live was foraged and hunted
in the lush green forests
that covered the land.
Always with respect for bird
animal, plant, tree and land.
Then followed those who wished to
own and dominate.
So started the battles
and the winner was the lord.
But even then the castle
was of local stone
food and clothing still
foraged and hunted in the forest.
But ever restless
man progressed to own more and more,
even striving to acquire ownership
of the entire land.
As wealth became a measure
so did what a man could own.

All the while man's ingenuity
created what looked like
God's answer to easy living.
Bit by bit as lush forests
dwindled cement jungles grew.
But still the countryside was there,
until many children grew to view
the country as a curiosity
to visit or see from the car.
For all we need we go to town
With growing vegetables and fruit
an experimental experience.

127. God Bless

God bless my love
your going is so painful,
you are my strength,
my reason to live.
my every thought and deed
will be guided by my love for you
until we meet again tonight.

My heart is filled with love,
and over flowing with joy
to see your smiling face,
with your eyes so full of love,
you make me so complete
when in the sweet security
of your loving arms.

128. World War

The world is in the throes of a war
the likes of which have never been witnessed
in the entire history of man,
no bombs or guns,
but all in the guise of love and smiles,
Satan has infiltrated every sphere of life,
and inch by inch like the slow rising tide
Satan's insidious evil
has swamped every cell of society,
from the lowest levels and youngest age
to the top ranks of government and Church
and all in between,
with the most insidious of Satan's baits – lust.
So from pornography to sexuality
the list for lust is endless,
the carrot is sins of the flesh,
with the unborn baby dehumanized
to the point of not being
eligible to be treated as more than a clump of cells
and the ending of the precious lives seen
as loving and caring for the women
who were blessed to be their mothers.

And while the world is being swamped
With the slimy suffocating sludge
There are those who gasp for air

And desperately try to make sense
Of where the world has gotten to,
And how to find the way back
Before the tide engulfs all.

129. The Old Woman

There was an old woman of dubious renown
who always wore a frown
her dog killed her cat
the old woman said 'that's that'
and with a very cross face
flew into outer space
there she got hit by a rock
it was such a hard knock
she dropped nice as could be
with a splash into the sea.

130. Who Tells

Who tells the worms to wiggle,
and the snake to slither,
the magpie to eat dead animal guts.
In Autumn who tells the mouse
it's warmer in my house,
and the squirrel to gather nuts,.
Who tells the bug to suck my blood,
and the rat that the sewer
is the place to live,
the caterpillar that cabbage
is where they will get fat,
who tells the cat to meow,
and the dog to bark,
the duck to swim,
and the lark to sing,
who tells the wren
whether it is a cock or a hen,
the calf to suck,
and the goat to puck,
who tells the bee
where to get the pollen,
and how to make the honey,
who tells the chick
to open wide its beak,
to get food from its mammy,

and who tells it to flap its wings,
who tells the robin
to gather moss to build a nest,
and who tells where it's best,
who tells the swallows
when it's time to gather on my clothes line
in readiness to fly to a warmer clime.
Who gives every bird animal and insect
their beauty grace and ingenuity
and what to do from first breath to death?
Let our every moment be filled
with grateful appreciation
for the intelligence and generosity of the
One Who created all
And remember who are we to threaten.

131. You Have An Angel

You have your own very special angel
always there with you
every waking and sleeping moment of the day,
every step you take and every word you speak,
someone who knows your every
thought hurt and hope
and if you open wide your heart
and treasure this precious presence
life's dips will be lightened
and pleasures and joys heightened.

132. The Wind

It knocked on the door and tapped on the windows,
it even howled down the chimney,
saying please, please come out to play,
it was oh so agile and feisty
as it hopped and skipped here and there.
It was strong and determined as it bent the trees,
whistling as it went through the reeds,
with a rippling chuckle it passed
through the long grass.
Its flowing robes billowed and bubbled
as it whooshed and whished and whirred,
going this way and that round and round the house,
"See, see" it would say we can have such fun.
Just then it roared like a tiger as it went up the hill,
it even tried to waken the great oak tree,
it tried and tried until the great oak groaned,
"Go away wind my leaves are shed and I'm asleep".
It teased the still water of the sea
and teased until it was as furious as could be,
making waves that were sky high.
I put on my woolly cap and went to join the wind
it blew me this way and that
and nearly stopped my breath,
it picked up leaves and bits of paper
and sent them swirling in the air,
I tried to catch them but the wind was too quick.

133. The Shoes

The lady was ever so pretty
and her feet were small and petite
and on them she elegantly wore
shoes of the softest red leather

But the shoes were not happy
and they could well recall

Being in the shoe shop
with shoes and boots sandals and slippers
of every colour style and make
neatly stacked in boxes and tastefullly displayed

But the shoes were not happy
and they could well recall

Being in the shoe factory
pieces of leather of every colour and shape
sewn together by busy machinists
and lovingly soled by shoemakers

But the shoes were not happy
and they could well recall

Being in the leather factory
hanging from hooks
great sheets of hide
being scrubbed and cured and coloured

But the shoes were not happy
and they could well recall

Being cows in a field
eating fresh green grass
and drinking cool clear water
feeling the sun and rain and hearing the birds

And oh they were so happy
and a bit of them would always be there.

134. The Swallow

Today I watched a swallow
flying gracefully through the air
dipping in a rhythmic flow.
Its slender body and delicate wings
belie the amazing strength
it takes to fly the endless miles
to find warm sunshine
while we wrap against the cold,
then with lengthening days
back the swallow comes
to herald another summer in our land,
what dynamo drives the tiny brain
to make the perilous trip
what intelligence makes
this little creature see
the advantage of seasonal change,
what wisdom prompts
the time to move
and when on the wing
how does this amazing
little creature eat and sleep?

135. Water

Water is God's most precious gift
to man and earth.
it flows, falls, swamps, seeps and floods.
But without it our world
would be a scorched barren plain,
no grass, no trees, no flowers, no fruit,
no birds, bees, cows, fish or elephants,
no soil, no clouds or sea shore
and of course no us.
Diamonds the biggest player in earthly wealth,
fade into insignificance
beside this shimmering sparkling
staff of all life,
honoured since time began,
and now seriously endangered by man.
What will it serve us
to have day trips to the moon
if every drop we drink is suspect.
Polluted by
the sum of all burnt fossil fuels
and other noxious fumes
that rise to rain on all we eat and drink,
the water from the crystal mountain stream,
the vast expanse of oceans,
the rain that falls from the sky

and the underground stream,
bear the brunt of man's advances.
Ingeniously we conserve, meter,
bottle, filter and purify,
moving ever further from water as it was.
Can we win the race?
Can we keep ahead of the poisonous waste?

136. Before We Go

If I thought for an instant when I casually say
good-bye, good luck or cheerio,
they were my last words to you,
I would hold you, hug you and kiss you,
and tell you how much I love you.
From my heart I would pour all the emotions
of joy, pride and appreciation
of all you are and ever were.
From the bottom of my heart also
I would ask you to forgive me
anything I ever did to cause you hurt,
pain or sadness,
and I would like you to know
that though it may not always
have been your perception,
everything I did was motivated by love
within the limits of my human frailty.
So now that you know
I would ask you to cherish this cameo
and hope we have many years
before it is time for either of us to go.

137. Our Loved Ones

Our loved ones' warm endearing smiles
beam down from heaven
enveloping us like downy soft angel wings,
protecting us against the pain of their going
and how things are here below.
Their love like rosebuds fills our space
leaving no room for painful thoughts
of how it might have been.
Their home is now in heaven,
it's there we send our love.
In our hearts we store our precious memories
and pray that time will heal the hurt.

138. Thank You God

I thank you God
for all I've done,
for every hurt I've ever had,
all the joy that's been mine
and the guiding spirit
that brought me on the road
to where I am.

Haiku

Silently dawn creeps
full of surprise the sun peeps,
a new day begun

****

Two people in love
another new life begun,
blessed be God above
******** Yesterday is gone
tomorrow has not yet come,
today is what is

****

We're born helpless babes
ride life's undulating waves,
and land on God's shore

****

It's not that we can't
we just haven't found out how,
go to it and try

****

We are what we are
because of what we do and say,
there is another way

****

Today is the day
on which we build our tomorrow,
be sure it's the best

****

Fruits quietly fall,
days grow short and nights long,
spirits call the soul

****

Fresh green shoots unfurl
so spring can't be far behind,
time of life and hope

****

Great oak spreads wide
roots burrow deep into earth,
all from one acorn
******* Sheep quietly graze
in their bellies lambs growing,
destined for slaughter

****

The thrush sweetly sings
with such varied range and tone,
joy fills our hearts

****

Yellow gorse blazes
brightening the countryside,
what creative skill?

****

The sun shines brightly
casting shadows long and clear,
a new day is born

****

The sun shines brightly
warming the earth air and sea,
giving us life

****

The caterpillar
has become a chrysalis,
soon to be a butterfly

www.ingramcontent.com/pod-product-compliance
Lightning Source LLC
Chambersburg PA
CBHW021628120626
46545CB00002B/443